Author:
Kathryn Senior is a former biomedical research scientist who studied at Cambridge University for a degree and a doctorate in microbiology. After 4 years in research she joined the world of publishing as an editor of children's science books. She has now been a full-time science writer for 10 years.

Artist:
David Antram was born in Brighton in 1958. He studied at Eastbourne College of Art and then worked in advertising for 15 years before becoming a full-time artist. He has illustrated many children's non-fiction books.

Series creator:
David Salariya was born in Dundee, Scotland. He has illustrated a wide range of books and has created and designed many new series for publishers both in the U.K. and overseas. In 1989 he established The Salariya Book Company. He lives in Brighton with his wife, the illustrator Shirley Willis, and their son Jonathan.

Editor:
Karen Barker Smith

Assistant Editor:
Stephanie Cole

Created, designed and produced by
The Salariya Book Company Ltd
Book House
25 Marlborough Place,
Brighton BN1 1UB

Please visit the Salariya Book Company at:
www.salariya.com

Published in Great Britain in 2002 by Hodder Wayland, an imprint of Hodder Children's Books

A catalogue record for this book is available from the British Library.

ISBN 0 7502 3599 3

Printed and bound in Belgium

Hodder Children's Books
A division of Hodder Headline Limited
338 Euston Road, London NW1 3BH

You Wouldn't Want to Be ILL in Tudor Times!

Written by
Kathryn Senior

Illustrated by
David Antram

You might feel just a little twinge...

Diseases you'd rather not catch

Created and designed by
David Salariya

HODDER
Wayland

an imprint of Hodder Children's Books

Contents

Introduction

You are called Nicholas Knight and you are a barber surgeon in Tudor times. You were born in 1533, the same year as Elizabeth I. Cities and towns in Tudor times are overcrowded and filthy, with animals living in houses and waste slopped straight into the street outside. It is no great surprise that people often get ill. When they do, there are no hospitals and doctors with a choice of medicines. The medicine around is weird and sometimes horrifying.

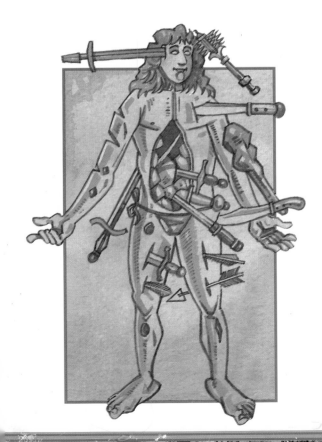

Your father was keen for you to be an important man in society and, as you showed an early interest in learning, you were sent to London at the age of 12 to become a barber surgeon's apprentice. London was an exciting place but, as you began to learn the craft of medicine from your master, you soon learnt why you wouldn't want to be ill in Tudor times!

A tough start

You first go to London to work with your master in 1545, when you are 12 years old. You have to share a room in your master's house with another young apprentice. The days are long and you spend them reading your master's books and listening to him talk about his work. After a few weeks, he decides to take you out to see the sick.

One way to diagnose illnesses in Tudor times is to examine patients' urine. For this purpose, your master has a collection of glass pots. You examine the urine three times: once when it is fresh, again when it has cooled for about an hour and, lastly, when it is completely cold. Sometimes you even have to taste the urine to see if it is sweet or sour!

You will need:

GLASS POTS in which to examine the urine; these are shaped like a bladder. You hold the pot up to the light to see its colour and to see if it contains any particles. You then consult a book (below) to make a diagnosis.

A COLOUR WHEEL that you use to compare the colour of the urine. The colours are linked to different types of illness.

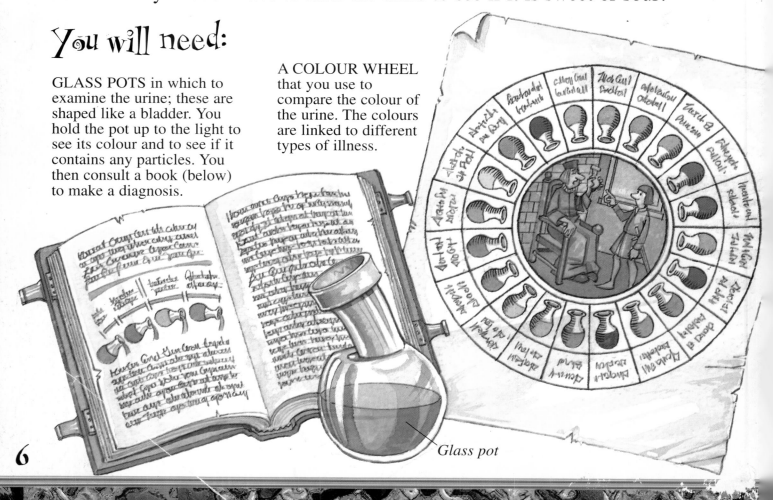

Glass pot

Padua - centre of learning

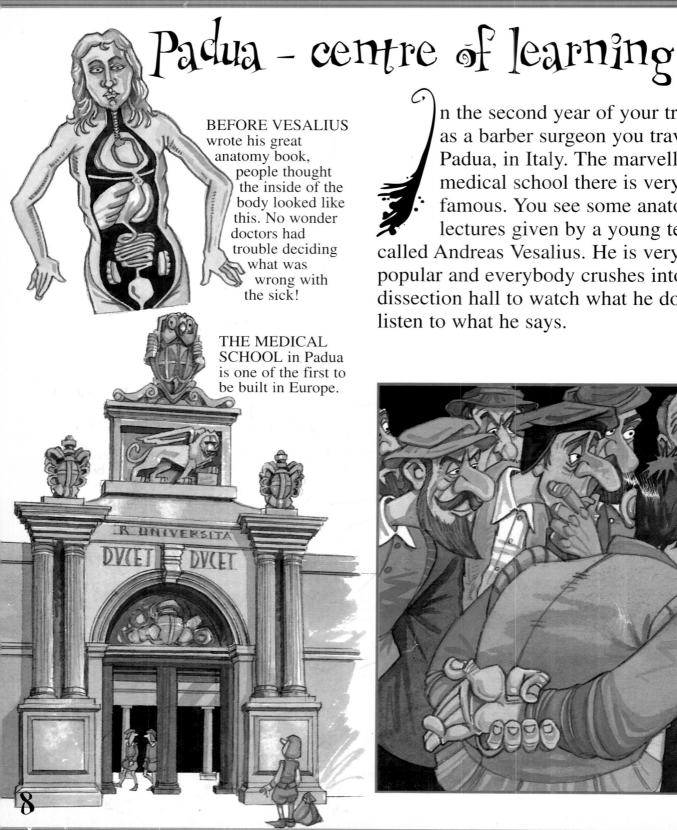

BEFORE VESALIUS wrote his great anatomy book, people thought the inside of the body looked like this. No wonder doctors had trouble deciding what was wrong with the sick!

THE MEDICAL SCHOOL in Padua is one of the first to be built in Europe.

In the second year of your training as a barber surgeon you travel to Padua, in Italy. The marvellous medical school there is very famous. You see some anatomy lectures given by a young teacher called Andreas Vesalius. He is very popular and everybody crushes into the dissection hall to watch what he does and listen to what he says.

Seeing a body being cut open and peeled apart piece by piece is both exciting and frightening. You have never seen anything like this in London. Vesalius has been working on his own book about anatomy and you find a copy of it in the library. The drawings show what is inside the body in great detail. It looks so strange; you can hardly believe all of it is inside you.

Handy hint

Get an artist with a strong stomach to draw from dissections. You don't want them to faint or be sick halfway through and only draw part of the body.

VESALIUS starts a strong tradition of anatomy at Padua. Eventually, a circular lecture theatre will be built (below), especially designed to avoid the crush and let everyone get a good view.

Blood glorious blood!

What you will need:

A 'MAP' of the veins of the body, showing the best points to get blood.

Barber surgeons think that illness is caused by 'badness' in the blood. They believe that letting the 'badness' out of the body will cure the patient. One of their main treatments is therefore blood-letting. The barber surgeon uses special tools to cut open a vein and then catches the blood in a shallow bowl. If you are not actually that ill, losing a little blood probably does no harm. The problem is that barber surgeons don't know when to stop. Many patients die from their treatment, after losing several pints of blood. A gentler method is to use leeches.

SEVERAL KNIVES and puncture pins for cutting into different veins. These are all sharpened regularly.

Handy hint

Slither

Make sure that you stop the bleeding and remove all the leeches before you leave. You don't want your patient to bleed to death from your treatment.

WHEN YOU ARE 14, you have the terrifying experience of going to the Royal Court with your master to treat Henry VIII. Despite the bleeding you do, and the rest and herbal potions your master precribes, the King dies at the end of January. You're sad the old King is dead, but glad that you don't have to go back there again!

Here we go again...

OOOOOwww!

Quick, lad - catch!

11

When humour wasn't funny

Alternative cures:

PUTTING A SOOTHING LOTION on the weapon that has wounded a soldier will, some people believe, cure that soldier instantly.

ASTROLOGY is widely used by Tudor doctors. They ask for a patient's birth sign and then make a diagnosis according to the position of the stars.

TOADS held next to a wart will cure the nasty hard lump of skin very quickly, according to the Tudors.

Croak

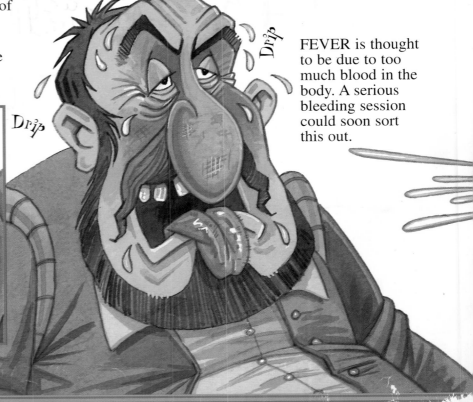

Drip

Drip

In Tudor times, people use the word 'humour' to describe the fluids that make up the human body. They believe the theories of a doctor called Galen who lived in ancient Greece. He said that the normal healthy person has four humours in their body: blood, phlegm, black bile and yellow bile. Blood is hot and wet; phlegm is cold and wet; black bile is cold and dry; yellow bile is hot and dry. According to Galen, when all four are present in equal amounts, the body is healthy. When they are out of balance, you become ill.

FEVER is thought to be due to too much blood in the body. A serious bleeding session could soon sort this out.

A DRY, HACKING COUGH with a fever is caused by too much yellow bile in the body.

Handy hint

Bad tempered patients often have too much hot blood. Give them regular blood lettings to calm them down.

SADNESS AND DEPRESSION are caused by an excess of black bile.

COLDS occur when you have too much phlegm in your body.

Battlefield horrors

One of the worst places to be in Tudor times is in the middle of a war. In 1563, you are made a barber surgeon in an army fighting in northern France. Soldiers face guns and muskets as well as swords, arrows, pikes and axes. The injuries suffered are horrendous, and barber surgeons like yourself can do very little. Conditions are filthy and there are no antiseptics. Limbs damaged in battle usually become infected and have to be amputated. Several people have to hold the soldier down. Even though he is given a whack on the head from the surgeon's mallet to knock him out, he will suffer tremendous pain. Few survive long after this dreadful ordeal.

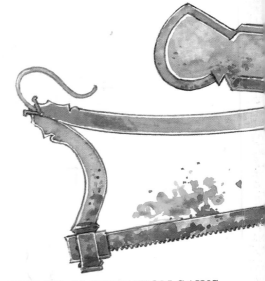

TUDOR AMPUTATION SAWS are designed to look decorative rather than to amputate limbs properly. Instruments are not washed between operations and are often dropped in the mud.

BARBER SURGEONS study battlefield wounds and draw diagrams to show all the ones that are possible (right).

15

Plagued by infections

Other nasty diseases:

ST VITUS' DANCE is a disease caused by a bacterial infection. It causes people to jerk and move uncontrollably, as if they are trying to do a wild dance.

LEPROSY is common in Tudor times. This disease eats away at skin and muscle. Because leprosy is easy to spot, lepers are outcasts and are forced to live away from other people.

SCROFULA is a form of tuberculosis. It can be cured, so it is said, by touching royalty. Touching a coin that the monarch has touched is also thought to work.

The Black Death, the largest ever outbreak of the plague, happened in the mid 1300s. It killed most of the population of Europe and then returned again and again. There is yet another bad outbreak in 1563 and many people leave London. Even Elizabeth I flees to Windsor with her household. To prevent the infection reaching her, she gives an order that anyone arriving at Windsor from London should be hung.

POP

There is little that you can do for somebody with either the spitting plague or the bubonic plague. Spitting plague makes you cough and spit blood and finishes you off in about 3 days. Bubonic plague causes huge boil-like lumps called buboes to erupt all over your body. Many die from it in about 5 days, but if you are still alive after that, you could recover.

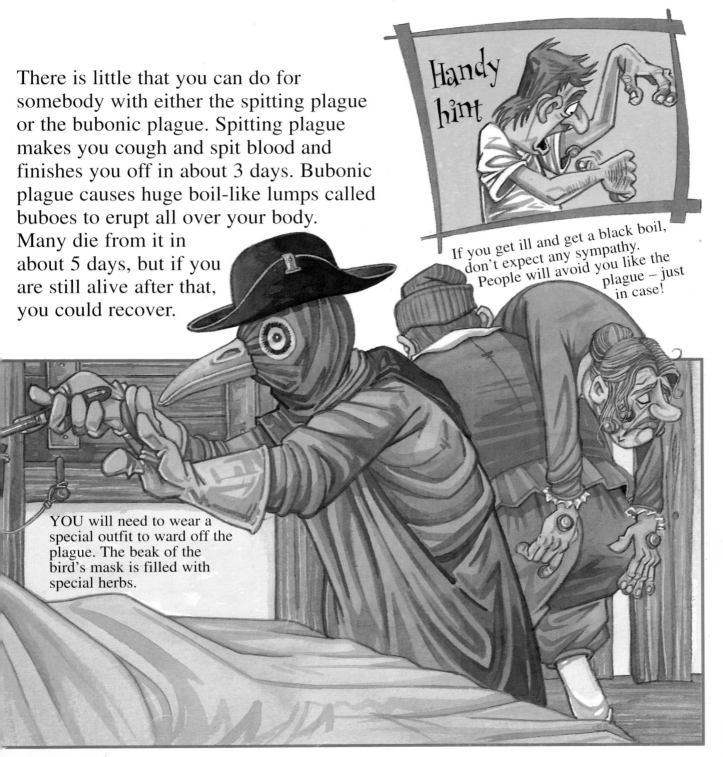

Handy hint

If you get ill and get a black boil, don't expect any sympathy. People will avoid you like the plague – just in case!

YOU will need to wear a special outfit to ward off the plague. The beak of the bird's mask is filled with special herbs.

Hospital surgery

After your time with the army, you return to England and take a position at St. Bartholomew's hospital in London. Most hospitals are places of fear in Tudor times. Usually only the poor go to them but they are forced to pay the hospital their funeral expenses before they are allowed in! The latest techniques are practised at St. Bartholomew's: nose jobs, tooth extractions and cataract operations. High-born soldiers who return from battle with injuries can get false limbs or a false nose made of gold. Some nobles have their noses altered to improve their appearance – an early form of plastic surgery.

False limbs:

TREPANNING is still carried out by Tudor barber surgeons. If you keep getting headaches, you may well have a hole drilled into your skull to let the 'badness' out.

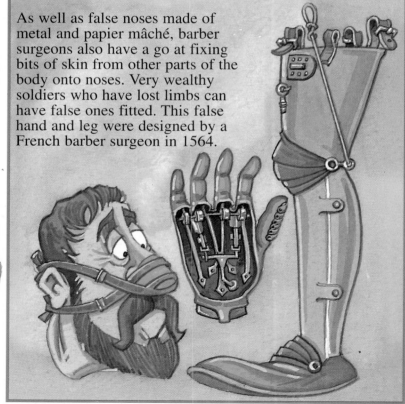

As well as false noses made of metal and papier mâché, barber surgeons also have a go at fixing bits of skin from other parts of the body onto noses. Very wealthy soldiers who have lost limbs can have false ones fitted. This false hand and leg were designed by a French barber surgeon in 1564.

19

Quacks and witches

The well-off in Tudor times can afford the services of a physician or a barber surgeon, but most people are too poor. Qualified doctors are also in short supply. This leaves things open for quacks, people who sell all sorts of potions and liquors that are supposed to cure everything. Many of them sell their cure-alls at fairs and by the side of the road and most people are taken in and buy them by the bottle-full. Barber surgeons hate quacks, but the sad truth is that the barber surgeon's medicines and potions are just as likely to fail. Neither man really has the knowledge to treat many illnesses.

Bottles of potion

Accused of witchcraft?

Maybe I should have drowned.

Guaranteed to make you live 'til you're 90!

WOMEN who make herbal remedies from the plants around them are often accused of witchcraft. The test for a witch is to bind the woman in a sack, or put her on a ducking stool, and then throw her in a river. If she floats, she is a witch. If she sinks, she is not. Women proved to be witches are then burned at the stake.

Herbs and the apothecary

JOHN GERARD grows his own herbs and writes a famous book on herbalism. Several other herbalists also publish books during the 1500s.

Apothecaries and herbalists become very important during Tudor times and you work with several of them. You meet John Gerard, one of the greatest herbalists of the time. He is himself a surgeon and has travelled widely. He grows over 1000 plants to treat his patients and will eventually publish his own guide to herbal medicine in 1597.

John Gerard boils different herbs in oil and extracts their essence. He rubs these highly fragrant oils into the skin of patients. You often ask John to make up herbal treatments. One of them – willow bark – is used as a treatment for pain. Willow bark turns out to contain a very potent ingredient that does actually dull pain.

Barbaric births

What you might need:

A BIRTHING CHAIR has a large hole in the seat for the baby to pass through. The long skirts of the mother are draped around the chair for modesty.

FORCEPS can pull a baby out, but in unskilled hands they can cause severe injuries, so be careful!

You might not want to be ill in Tudor times, but it is also a good idea not to be a woman. Girls marry at very young ages – 12 or 13 – and then have children constantly. Childbirth is dangerous. Many women die in labour or after birth because of infection. Many babies also die.

AAARGGHH!

Only noble women are attended by a barber surgeon. If things go wrong, you could use forceps to pull the baby out. Your knowledge of anatomy also encourages you to carry out a caesarean, an operation to remove a baby from its mother.

Handy hint

Tell every pregnant patient that you have that she should make arrangements for the baby's birth, and for its funeral, just in case.

Perhaps it's time to use the knife.

Congratulations!

MIDWIVES attend women giving birth and look after them afterwards. They aren't trained, but they learn from other midwives and generally they do a good job.

25

At war again – the Armada

Between 1577 and 1580, you are the barber surgeon on the *Golden Hind*, the ship captained by Sir Francis Drake. Sailors are often ill. They are always wet, and they barely sleep on the boards below deck. Their diet of salt pork, beef, cheese, dried fish and biscuits gives them scurvy.

In 1588, you are barber surgeon on Drake's ship during the Spanish Armada. On 21 July, Francis Drake attacks the Armada near Plymouth. The Armada is beaten but the cost to sailors is high. Many suffer terrible injuries after being shot or trapped behind cannons.

Splash!

Scurvy

Scurvy is caused by not eating enough vitamin C, but the Tudors don't know that. You find that some herbs help, particularly when eaten fresh.

End of an era

After the success of the Armada, your bravery is recognised by the Queen, Elizabeth I. She makes you one of her personal physicians for the last 5 years of her life. This is not always a pleasant experience – she becomes bad tempered and bitter as she gets older. In February 1603 you are called to her. She has been walking in the cold air and has caught a chill. For two weeks you go to her every day, advising rest and giving hot infusions of different herbs.

ARCHBISHOP WHITGIFT, the Archbishop of Canterbury, is the only man that Elizabeth I wants with her as she is dying. Her doctors are all turned away.

Go away – you can do nothing for me now.

However, in mid March, the Queen decides never to see any of her doctors again. She lies on cushions, hardly eating or drinking. You call for another week, but are refused an audience. Elizabeth falls into a deep sleep and on the morning of 24th March 1603, she dies. The Tudor age has ended.

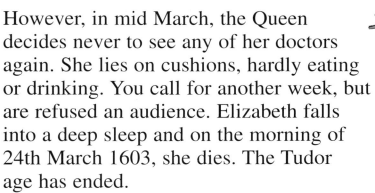

Handy hint
A new fashion for smoking has just begun. Avoid this at all costs as it is particularly bad for your health.

YOU TEACH a group of apprentices during the last 15 years of your career, just as your master did 50 years ago. You die at the age of 72, a grand old age for someone who has spent his life mixing with the sick and ill of Tudor times.

See what it says about an orangey colour.

Glossary

Amputation Cutting off someone's limb – usually their leg.

Anatomy The branch of science that is to do with the structure of the body, including the bones in the skeleton, how the muscles are attached to them, and what the major organs are like.

Antiseptic A substance that kills germs.

Apprentice Someone who is learning a craft, trade or profession.

Astrology Foretelling the future by looking at the positions of the stars.

Barber surgeon A general doctor who treated the sick in Tudor times, doing minor operations and recommending herbal potions. So called because before Tudor times, this role was taken by a man who also cut hair, trimmed beards and extracted teeth.

Bile A green, bitter liquid produced by a small gland just below the liver.

Bladder The small bag inside the body that stores urine. Urine is produced in the kidneys, and it passes to the bladder for storage.

Cataract A milky skin that forms on the eyes, particularly in older people. It can cause blindness.

Diagnosis Identification of a patient's illness by looking at their symptoms.

Dissection Cutting up the body to study the structure of what is inside.

Ducking stool A low stool attached to a frame. In Tudor times, a form of punishment was to be put on the stool and ducked underneath the water of a lake or pond.

Essence Essences of plants and flowers were obtained by boiling them up and then concentrating the resulting liquid.

Fever An illness that causes the temperature of the body to rise. Severe fevers can be very dangerous, and can lead to fits or even death.

Herbalism Treating illness using mixtures and preparations of herbs.

Infusion An infusion was prepared by boiling a plant or herb. It was then given to the patient as a health-giving drink.

Leeches Small, slug-like animals that suck blood.

Mallet A blunt hammer that surgeons used to knock out patients that needed serious surgery, such as a leg amputation.

Midwife A woman who looks after a woman in labour (having a baby).

Musket A type of gun used in Tudor times.

Opium A drug made from poppies.

Phlegm The gooey substance produced by the lungs and linings of the nose and throat when a person has a cold or other infection.

Pike A long, spear-like weapon used by soldiers in Tudor times.

Plague A disease spread by rats that caused many deaths during the 14th, 15th and 16th centuries.

Posy A bunch of pleasant smelling flowers that many people carried around. Tudor times were very smelly, and when it got too much, you could smell your posy.

Potent Very powerful.

Remedy A treatment in Tudor times was often called a remedy. It was an early form of a medicine.

Trepanning The practice of cutting a hole in the skull to let out evil spirits.

Urine The liquid produced by the kidneys and lost from the body when we go to the loo.

Index